21ST
CENTURY
DEBATES

VIOLENCE IN SOCIETY

THE IMPACT ON OUR LIVES

RONDA ARMITAGE

Raintree

Chicago, Illinois

21st Century Debates Series

Genetics • Surveillance • The Internet • The Media • Artificial Intelligence • Climate Change • Energy • Rain Forests • Waste, Recycling, and Reuse • Endangered Species • Air Pollution • An Overcrowded World? • Food Supply • Water Supply • World Health • Global Debt • Terrorism • The Drug Trade • New Religious Movements • Racism • Tourism • Globalization • Transportation

© 2004 Raintree

Published by Raintree, a division of Reed Elsevier Inc., Chicago, Illinois

For information, address the publisher:
Raintree, 100 N. LaSalle, Suite 1200, Chicago, IL 60602

Printed in Hong Kong by Wing King Tong.
08 07 06 05 04
10 9 8 7 6 5 4 3 2 1

Library of Congress Cataloging-in-Publication Data
Armitage, Ronda.
  Violence in society / Ronda Armitage.
    p. cm. -- (21st century debates)
Includes bibliographical references and index.
Contents: A violent world -- Family violence -- Violence in young people's lives -- Violent crime -- Racism and violence -- Political violence -- Violence as entertainment -- Preventing violence.
  ISBN 0-7398-6469-6 (library binding)
 1. Violence. 2. Violent crimes. 3. Family violence. 4. Racism. 5. Political violence. [1. Violence. 2. Violent crimes. 3. Family violence. 4. Racism. 5. Political violence.] I. Title. II. Series.
  HM1116.A76 2004
  306.874'3--dc21
                    2003009694

Picture acknowledgments: Camera Press 43; Howard Davies/Exile Images 8, 15, 32, 44, 58 and cover background; HWPL 40; Impact Photos 23 (Peter Arkell); Popperfoto 5, 7 above (Yannis Behrakis), 7 below and 26 (Corinne Dufka), 12, 27 (David van der Veen), 28 (Saeed Khan), 35, 37, 41, 42, 47 (Aditia), 48 (Gil Cohen Magen), 53 and cover foreground (Philippe Laurenson), 54 (Steve Marcus), 55 (Emilio Morenatti), 57; Rex Features 29 (Denis Cameron), 30, 34 (A. Krause), 46; Topham 4, 10 and 36 (Bob Daemmrich/The Image Works), 12, 13 (Eastcott/Momatiuk/The Image Works), 16, 17, 19 (Peter Hvizdak/The Image Works), 20, 21, 25, 33, 39, 50, 52.

Cover: foreground picture shows British soccer fans clashing with French teens in Marseilles in 1998; background picture shows weapons confiscated in Cambodia.

Every effort has been made to trace copyright holders. However, the publishers apologize for any unintentional omissions and would be pleased in such cases to add an acknowledgment in any future editions.

CONTENTS

A VIOLENT WORLD

Violent by nature?

Since ancient times the world has been a violent place where many people have had to fight to survive. Human beings are unique as a species, in that we will fight and kill even when our survival does not depend on it. We will use violence to gain dominance over other individuals, groups or nations for personal, racial, religious, or economic advantage.

Violence is a part of all our lives. Some of us have been victims of violence ourselves, or know someone who has. In addition, television, radio, and newspaper reports of wars, murders, rapes, and child abuse make us all aware of the violence that exists in the world. This violence in society affects all of us in one way or another, from ordinary citizens being afraid to go out at night to parents worrying about children walking to their own to school.

It is difficult to know whether violence in all its forms is more common today than it used to be. Keeping crime statistics is a relatively recent phenomenon. Figures are not available for violence in, for example, 14th-century Europe. However, we like to think of ourselves as more civilized than our ancestors, so most of us find violent behavior extremely shocking and offensive. Certainly there

Violence has always been part of humankind's struggle to survive. This artist's impression shows our prehistoric ancestors, about 20,000 years ago, trapping a woolly mammoth in a specially dug pit and killing it with stone weapons.

is a widespread belief, even among people with a fairly high standard of living, that crime, particularly violent crime, is on the increase.

Defining violence

"Violence: physically aggressive behaviors that do, or potentially could, cause injury or death." Although dictionary definitions of violence vary, most emphasize the physical aspects of the act. But it is possible to define violence more broadly than that. For instance, violence can be psychological: a person may be mentally damaged by repeated cruelty or threats. Sexual abuse and rape also usually involve coercion (forcing someone to do something they don't want to do, often in order to avoid further harm). Children and adults exposed to all sorts of violent situations, such as long-term family violence or war, sometimes suffer from post-traumatic stress disorder, which can affect both their physical and their mental health for a long period of time.

VIEWPOINT

"Violence is: Anger, pain, absence of reason, pressure, control (mental and emotional), belittling someone, a release of tension, big risk, fear, power, hatred, showing emotions, self-defense, domination of another, bullying."
Young prisoners in a violence group, 2000

Terrified Roman Catholic children are shielded by parents and police officers during violent protests as they make their way to Holy Cross Primary School in North Belfast, Ireland, in September 2001.

What makes people violent?

All of us have sometimes become angry or seen others in a violent mood. We may feel aggressive, but usually our violence remains a feeling. It does not result in violent behavior.

So why are some individuals more aggressive, and why do they actually commit violent acts? Explanations have varied over time. For example, in the 1800s the Italian psychiatrist Cesare Lombroso suggested that people inherited the criminal gene. In other words, he believed it had nothing to do with their upbringing or experience of life—criminals were born, not made. Later it was thought that certain inherited psychological traits, such as dishonesty or the inability to meet other people's needs, made individuals more likely to turn to crime and violence. In the 20th century, these ideas were replaced by theories emphasizing the role of social factors such as poverty, inequality, and family upbringing, and crime statistics seem to support these theories. For instance there is relatively less crime in prosperous, democratic countries, such as Sweden, Norway, and Japan. These are countries with a relatively small gap between rich and poor and with less social inequality between classes.

Violence in war

War is the most devastating violence that human beings inflict on each other. The 20th century, with two world wars, saw more humans killing other humans than all previous centuries combined. All weapons of war are designed to kill, but 20th-century advances in science and technology have generated new kinds of warfare that enable the greatest amount of damage to be done from the farthest distance. Much of the fighting against terrorists in Afghanistan in 2001, for instance, was conducted from the air, using bombs and missiles to search out enemy targets.

Major weapons of mass destruction, such as nuclear bombs, destroy all life and property for miles around and leave the area contaminated with radiation for years to come.

The vast majority of wars during recent years have been civil wars. These wars have not only caused millions of deaths but also triggered a worldwide refugee crisis, because people have left their villages and countries to escape the fighting.

A U.S. Air Force B-52 carpet bombs the Taliban positions northwest of Kabul, Afghanistan, in October 2001. The B-52s pounded the hardline Islamic movement in some of the heaviest strikes of the campaign.

A survivor of a massacre of Tutsi refugees holds her two children in a temporary camp that has been set up to protect them. More than 270 civilians were killed during the attack on the Tutsi refugee camp in northwest Rwanda. The killings were carried out by Hutu militias during the civil war in Rwanda in 1994.

FACT

In 1995, the world's 225 richest people had a combined wealth of over $1 trillion. Only 4 percent of this wealth, $40 billion, would be enough to pay for basic education, health care, adequate food, and safe water and sanitation for all.

Ethnic differences and poverty have been major factors in many civil wars. Political stability is largely dependent on economic stability, so the poorer the country, and the more deprived large sections of its population are, the greater the likelihood of large-scale unrest. Of the world's most indebted countries, twelve have suffered civil war or violent conflict in the last few decades. These countries are: Angola, Central African Republic, Comoros, Democratic Republic of the Congo, Ethiopia, Guinea-Bissau, Liberia, Sierra Leone, Somalia, Sudan, Uganda, and Mozambique.

A stockpile of weapons is confiscated by police in Cambodia. Many Cambodians have guns from the long years of war.

Is violence ever acceptable?

Whatever the dictionary says, in practice we may or may not describe certain acts as criminal or violent depending on our culture and the circumstances or period of history in which they occur. For example, during wars, all kinds of brutalities that at any other time would be regarded as cold-blooded murder are seen as both acceptable and necessary.

Even in everyday life there sometimes seems to be little logic in the way society deals with different forms of violence. Sweden, among other countries, has banned all corporal punishment of children. Meanwhile in Great Britain, and the United States, parents are still permitted to spank children. Yet if the same people spanked an adult they could be charged with assault. Throughout the world police and the legal system view domestic violence less seriously than violence by a stranger.

Furthermore, violence can be psychological as well as physical. For instance, workplace bullying (the abuse of power by a person in authority, such as an employer) is becoming an increasing problem. Workplace bullying has been described as offensive treatment through vindictive, cruel, or humiliating attempts to undermine an individual or group of employees. It occasionally takes the form of physical harassment but more often constant destructive criticism, humiliating personal remarks in front of colleagues, spreading gossip, and starting rumors.

Is violence inevitable?

There are some examples of nonviolent societies. For instance the Hutterites, a religious sect living in the United States and Canada had a classless society where economic resources were shared fairly equally. There were no murders and only one suicide in 100 years (1874–1974). Samoa, an island in the Pacific, also has very little crime, perhaps partly due to Samoans' strong sense of loyalty to their family, community, and church. In addition, very few Samoans experience poverty, and resources are usually shared equally.

> **FACT**
>
> During World War I, hundreds of British soldiers were killed by their own troops for refusing to engage in killing the enemy.

> **DEBATE**
>
> How would you define violence? Think about your own life and consider if and when you have ever experienced any violence.

FAMILY VIOLENCE

Happy families?

Most people throughout the world live at least part of their lives in a family group. Or they may be part of an extended family made up of grandparents, aunts, uncles, and cousins, as well as parents and children. For an increasing majority, family means a nuclear family—one or two parents or stepparents and their children living in a family home. Whatever the situation, the hope is that the adults will be happy and the children will be raised in a loving environment. However, the evidence suggests that there are a great many unhappy families.

Some families, like this one in Texas, enjoy life together. Other families are torn apart by conflict and violence.

Murder, assault, and sexual abuse are all more likely to be carried out by a member of the victim's family than by anyone else. Family violence (often known as domestic violence) is common throughout the world. And research shows that, although women and young children are most likely to be the victims, it can happen to any family member.

Family life involves more emotional intensity and personal intimacy than most other human relationships. Because family ties are often charged with strong, contradictory emotions, including both love and hate, a quarrel that breaks out in the home can spiral out of control more quickly than it would in another social setting, where the participants would have to modify their behavior because they are with other people. Family violence happens behind closed doors.

Children and family violence

The National Society for the Prevention of Cruelty to Children (NSPCC) defines child cruelty as "neglect, physical injury, sexual or emotional abuse inflicted or knowingly not prevented, which causes significant harm or death." While sexual abuse is disapproved of in all cultures, definitions of "neglect," "physical injury," and "emotional abuse" vary from culture to culture, and there are widely differing ideas on how children should be brought up. For instance, in some Indian families there is an emphasis on corporal punishment but this is seen as an expression of parental concern rather than hostility to the child. Traditional Chinese culture emphasizes the principle of filial devotion (or *xiao*). Children are expected to be absolutely obedient to their parents. In extreme cases this could even mean the child sacrificing his or her own life for the sake of the parents.

VIEWPOINT

"Such a mammoth problem requires swift and far-reaching action by Congress and the courts. Anything less would be both inadequate and an insult to the survivors and victims of violence."
Patricia Ireland, former president of the National Organization for Women, 2000

In Victorian Britain the children of the poor, particularly orphans, often experienced extreme hardship and abuse. These homeless boys were photographed in about 1880, when they were admitted to an orphanage run by a charity.

Who are the abusers?

For many children some form of violence is a part of their everyday lives because their abuser is another family member. A U.S. Bureau of Justice study showed that only one in seven convicted child abusers attacked a child they did not already know. One third had committed abuse against their own children. Mothers are just as likely as fathers to physically harm their children. The only violent crime where women exceed men is physical cruelty to children under four years old, perhaps because women are usually still the main caretakers of young children and babies and therefore spend more time with them.

However, child sexual abuse by women is rare. Men are the main abusers. There are many reasons why some adults take advantage of their authority over young people. Social factors, such as poverty and unemployment, create considerable stress for families who may be isolated within their community, without extended family or friends. The feeling of having no power within adult relationships, or having been abused as a child, may also play a part. Most adults who harm children experienced destructive childhoods themselves.

Protecting children

Countries in the developed world have laws to protect children from being harmed by adults. Various acts grant power to social services, the police, and other organizations to intervene to protect children at risk. In the most serious cases of harm, children will be taken into state care. In 1998 in Britain it was estimated that there were 200,000 children living away from home, either in residential institutions or in foster care. Legislation in many countries has also shifted the emphasis from parent's rights over a child to their duties and responsibilities toward the child.

Women as victims of violence

In 1981 the anthropologist David Levinson reported that the most common form of family violence throughout the world was wife beating. Until the 1800s women in most societies were seen as being owned by their husbands and therefore of lower status. Physical punishment was often used to keep women under control. A married woman's body, her property, her earnings, and her children all belonged to her husband.

FACT

Three out of four children who have been in long-term care (in children's homes or living with foster families) have no academic qualifications or employment when they leave their care homes or foster families. A third of young homeless people have been in state care, as have 40 percent of the young people in prison.

A young woman waits to be admitted to a domestic violence shelter.

VIEWPOINT

"...a wife batterer ... has learned that striking out against another relieves stress, helps him to feel powerful, masculine and in control. This coping mechanism is extremely destructive and hurtful to others."
Dr Paul Hanck, Calm Down, 1980

VIEWPOINTS

"Statistics reveal that 30 percent of women are regularly beaten by their husbands."
The Ministry of Social Affairs, Egypt, 2002

"So what? A woman's role is to obey her husband; if she does not then she deserves what she gets."
Cab driver, Cairo, Egypt, 2002

Although various laws passed over the last 150 years have changed the position of women in developed nations, the idea that they should obey and serve men still persists and, until relatively recently, the majority of crimes against women were not taken seriously. They were considered merely domestic disputes that occurred as a normal, acceptable part of any relationship.

Then, in 1994, the United States Congress passed the Violence Against Women Act. Three million dollars were set aside to reestablish a national helpline for victims and survivors of domestic abuse. The police were given better training in order to understand the issues involved in family violence, and more legal protection was provided for battered women. Similar laws and services have been established throughout Europe, New Zealand, and Australia.

Despite these developments, it has been estimated that, in the U.S., Britain, Australia, and New Zealand, one in four women lives in a violent relationship. Some 80 percent of all women murdered know their killer. The biggest single category of killer is a husband, partner, or ex-partner. Until 1991 rape within marriage was not recognized in Britain. A law then ruled that a husband has no right to force himself on his wife. During the 1990s there was an increase in the number of reported incidents where the victim knew the rapist. Relatives, friends, former partners, or recent aquaintances commit 43 percent of sexual assaults. A considerable portion of violent crime in the U.S. and Europe is domestic violence rather than violence at the hands of a stranger.

Women around the world
Change has taken place more slowly in other parts of the world. In regions such as Africa and Asia,

women often have lower status than men. Fewer educational and job opportunities are available to them so they remain more dependent on fathers or husbands for support. In 1990, Iraq passed an official order allowing men to kill their wives for adultery even if it was unproven.

India has a particular problem with dowry-related violence. If a newly married woman's husband is dissatisfied with the dowry (usually money or goods) provided by her family on their wedding day, she may be burned alive. Although dowries are now illegal in India, they are still common in rural areas. According to the Indian government, sixteen Indian women are killed each day in dowry burnings.

FACT

Violence by male partners is the single largest cause of injury to women worldwide— more than muggings and car accidents combined.

A 2001 poster helps create awareness about domestic violence in Cambodia. It is estimated that one in six Cambodian women are physically abused by their husbands.

FACT

About one-third of women murdered in the U.S. and Japan each year are killed by their husbands.

A 1992 report from Brazil noted that wife-murder is a common crime, and that men who commit wife-murder are often found not guilty because it is still acceptable to defend a man's honor by means of murder. For example, many Brazilians believe that a husband is completely within his rights to execute an unfaithful wife. The courts would see this as an act of self defense. And, because women are considered to belong to men, any attempt they make to protect themselves is seen as a threat to their husbands.

Men who batter

Men who abuse come from all walks of life, all classes, all races, and all ages. Some are violent only to their partners, not to anyone else. But over half those men who are violent to their partners also abuse their children. Some research suggests that the causes are social. From an early age it is considered more acceptable for boys to resolve issues by fighting. "Tough guy" images in movies and television may also contribute to the view men develop of themselves. Many will have learned violent behavior as children, either by being abused or humiliated, or by witnessing violence being used as a way of resolving conflict in their families. As adults, they often associate with men who have similar outlooks and so they continue to believe that such behavior is right. Men who feel powerless within a relationship may use violence as a means of trying to demonstrate power and control.

Primary school boys often play rough, whereas girls tend to spend more time talking. Are boys naturally more aggressive, or are they influenced by society's expectations of men?

Women and family violence

At the same time, men are increasingly becoming the victims of domestic violence. Those most likely to be attacked are in their early thirties, unmarried, but living with a woman. There are millions of assaults in the home each year, almost evenly split between male and female perpetrators. But male violence toward women is much more likely to result in death or lasting harm than women's violent acts toward men.

Parent abuse

Parents have a position of power and authority in a family and, within certain limits, it is assumed that they will decide how that power is used. Society shows considerable disapproval of children who are violent to their parents, yet parents are often blamed for their children's violent behavior.

Junior members of Umkhonto We Sizwe (the militant wing of the African National Congress) demonstrate their fighting skills at a 1993 rally in Soweto, South Africa.

FACT

During the Vietnam War, 58,000 American soldiers were killed. During the same period, between 30,000 and 54,000 American women were killed in their homes.

The jury in the trial of Lyle (right) and Erik Menendez, accused of murdering their wealthy Beverly Hills parents, found them guilty on both counts of murder even though they claimed to have been abused by their parents.

Research shows that older children and young adults do inflict injuries on their parents. For instance, in the United States about 10 percent of parents with a 10- to 17-year-old living at home will experience at least one violent act a year. Over 3 percent of these adolescents were reported to have kicked, punched, beaten up, or used a gun or knife against a parent. In extreme cases, children have killed a parent.

Elder abuse

Abuse toward the elderly is on the increase. In the developed world, better food, better health care, and improved living conditions have all contributed to an increase in the elderly population. Although many elderly people may remain in their own homes until they die, others need to be cared for. The rising cost of care in institutions means that a growing number of elderly people become the responsibility of their families. This may place increasing pressures on their adult children, in terms of accommodation, financial stress, or a restriction in lifestyle.

FACT

In 1994, in the 75 largest urban areas in the U.S., 2 percent of all murder victims were parents killed by their children.

Abusive treatment toward the elderly can take many forms. Caretakers may tie their elderly relatives to a bed while they go out shopping. Elderly people may be bullied into changing a will or handing over house deeds to the caretaker. Some elderly people are physically attacked and injuries can be easily dismissed as accidents. All these types of abuse can sometimes go unnoticed because the elderly are often isolated from the community and may find it difficult to report abusive incidents.

Violence in gay and lesbian relationships

One of the most overlooked forms of family violence is that in gay and lesbian relationships. During the 1970s and 1980s, discussion of "family violence" tended to focus solely on heterosexual relationships. The emphasis, too, was on domestic violence as something that men do to women. Prejudice about gay men and women stopped many victims of this form of family violence from speaking out. It was not until 1999 that legislation was passed in Britain ruling that a homosexual couple in a stable relationship could be defined as a family. Evidence now suggests that violence between homosexual couples is at least as great as that between heterosexual couples.

> **FACT**
>
> Only about 5 percent of elder-abuse complaints are made by the victims themselves. As with other forms of family violence, they often assume they are somehow to blame for the abuse. Sometimes, as an elderly parent, they are embarrassed to admit they have raised a child who is capable of such behavior. Often their love for the abuser is stronger than the desire to leave the abusive situation.

In developed countries people are living much longer than they used to, and the elderly can be very vulnerable to violence.

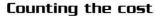

VIEWPOINT

"We need to cancel the hitting license in society. [We need] elimination of spanking as a child-rearing technique; gun control to get deadly guns out of the home; elimination of corporal punishment in school; elimination of the death penalty; and an elimination of media violence that glorifies ... violence. Reducing poverty, inequality, and unemployment and providing for adequate housing and medical care... and providing educational opportunities are steps that could reduce stress in families."

Richard Gelles, Intimate Violence in Families, *1997*

Counting the cost

Studies show that children who are abused live in constant fear, feeling powerless to take any action to stop the violence and abuse. Parents are unable to meet their children's needs and the children may become either increasingly withdrawn or more aggressive. In the long term, some of these children will find it difficult to trust people and form lasting relationships.

On the average, women will suffer an abusive relationship for six years before asking for help. The stress of living in these conditions can trigger a range of physical and mental illnesses in victims of family violence. These include depression, anxiety, eating problems, and post traumatic stress disorder.

The cost to society

It is very difficult to calculate the financial costs of family violence. There are medical and therapy bills for physical and emotional damage; prison costs for those convicted; the costs of running safe refuges for battered women; housing costs after separation and divorce; social services, police and court costs; the list goes on. Some estimates have been made, however. Violence against women is estimated to cost the U.S. economy as much as $67 billion annually, based on the costs of medical treatment, lost worker productivity, and quality of life. In 1999 British government agencies and charities spent about $1.6 billion on child abuse. Most of this money was spent on the consequences of abuse rather than its prevention.

A mother and her child find safety at a shelter for battered women in Tel Aviv, Israel.

Breaking the cycle

It is now widely recognized that violence and abuse are often part of a cycle of learned behavior. People who have experienced violence, particularly during

early childhood, are more likely to become violent themselves, either to their spouse or children or both. Fortunately, fewer than half those whose childhoods were violent continue the cycle, and there are a number of initiatives to prevent abused children from becoming abusive parents. For example, in Ontario, Canada, doctors working with problem fourteen- to sixteen-year-olds advise them on how to get medical and social help. The participants assist in social work projects and use role-play to work through their feelings. After several years, the doctors reported a three-fold decrease in violent behavior.

Women attend a counseling session at a battered women's shelter in Texas.

How do you think family members should handle conflict in order to reduce the chances of violence in the home?

VIOLENCE IN YOUNG PEOPLE'S LIVES

The rights of children

In November 1989 the United Nations adopted the Convention on the Rights of the Child. This Convention changed the obligations of all adults to children everywhere. Most importantly the 1989 Convention requires that children be safeguarded against all forms of abuse, neglect, and exploitation. Even though there have been some improvements in child protection since the Convention was passed, children remain the most vulnerable and powerless group in all societies.

Homelessness

In the industrialized world, most child abuse and neglect takes place within families. In extreme circumstances these children are removed to a safe place to ensure their survival. In recent years some have spent time in residential children's homes. Although many of these homes provide good standards of care, it has come to light that a few have been very abusive institutions that continued the cycle of abuse and violence.

Many cities in the developed world have increasingly large numbers of homeless people. Some young people who have experienced abusive family situations or family breakdown may either be forced to leave home or simply run away. The "youth homelessness" problem includes young people living on the streets as well as on friends' floors or in hostels. Others have mental health

FACT

Homeless people are nearly four times as likely to be murdered as the general population. The average life expectancy of a homeless person is only about 47 years.

A homeless young man begs in the street.

problems or go to the city hoping to find employment. Once people find themselves without a permanent address, it becomes very difficult to find work and their lives may deteriorate in a downward spiral of deprivation and hardship.

Many homeless people of all ages become victims of crime, and some commit crimes in order to survive. Most view themselves as outsiders in society, excluded from the everyday activities, such as going to work, being with friends, or keeping a bank account, that others take for granted.

Bullying
Most bullying takes place in school settings but it can occur wherever groups of children gather together. Both males and females bully, but their methods vary considerably. Boys tend to use name-calling and physical aggression, whereas girls are more likely to resort to psychological warfare to control their victims, usually other girls. This cruelty between girls has spread through schools very rapidly.

VIEWPOINT

"Being called names, being teased, being pushed or pulled around, being hit or attacked, having your bag or other possessions taken and thrown around, having rumors spread about you, being ignored and left out, being forced to hand over money or possessions, being attacked because of religion, race, or color."

Descriptions of bullying by children and young people

FACT

After the 1999 massacre at Columbine High School in Littleton, Colorado, when Eric Harris and Dylan Klebold shot and killed 15 people and injured 23 more, it was revealed that the two killers had been subjected to repeated taunting, teasing, insults, name-calling, and rejection.

FACT

In 1995 a little girl called Megan Kanka was raped and killed in New Jersey. Nine months later Megan's Law was introduced, allowing communities to access names and addresses of known sex offenders who are required by law to give their addresses to the police. Opponents of this policy argue that it only drives pedophiles, fearful of persecution by the public, to go into hiding. This makes it harder for the authorities to keep track of their whereabouts.

Although most schools now take bullying seriously, a third of all girls surveyed and a quarter of boys in 2000 said they had been too afraid to go to school at some time in their lives. A report on the long-term effects of bullying found that adults who had been bullied as children experienced problems in later life, including low self-esteem, suicidal thoughts, and difficulty relating to people. New ideas for making the bully accountable for his or her actions have been tried in many schools. In the state of Washington there is a school-based initiative called the Empower Program that enables bullies and people who are bullied to come together in a spirit of nonconfrontational honesty and openness.

Violent children

In February 1993 two-year-old James Bulger was murdered in Liverpool, Britain. Two ten-year-old boys were convicted of his murder and people were appalled that young boys could have committed such a horrendous act. Although little was heard about it at the trial, both boys had grown up in abusive households where they experienced neglect, bullying, and physical violence. These factors may well have contributed to the boys' extremely violent behavior. Despite the enormous media coverage of the Bulger case in Britain, murders by children are rare.

Pedophiles and the Internet

Most children grow up in a loving environment with parents who care for and protect them. However, growing awareness of child abuse, particularly abuse by strangers, has frightened many parents and discouraged them from allowing children the freedom experienced in earlier generations.

Although most children who are sexually abused know the person who abuses them, it is abuse by a stranger that arouses most fear. Pedophiles, who abduct and sexually abuse children, are seen as a particular threat. With the increased use of the Internet, some pedophiles have succeeded in getting to know their victims through chatrooms, perhaps by posing as children or teenagers. For example in 2000 a British pedophile was imprisoned for five years after he posed as a teenage boy and lured a thirteen-year-old girl to his home. The police and Internet providers continue to search for ways to trace suspected pedophiles.

Mothers of murdered children lead a march through central London in 1996, demanding more action to protect youngsters from pedophiles.

Children and war

In many developing countries, children face different dangers. About 600 million children are in families living on less than $1 per day. According to the charity Save the Children, an estimated 300,000 children, some as young as seven, are fighting in wars or conflicts in countries such as Mozambique, Colombia, Afghanistan, Angola, and Turkey. Most fighters are boys, but girls are also used. Many girls are sexually abused and forced to be the "wives" or unpaid servants of adult soldiers. Some children are kidnapped and made to fight. Others, who often come from very poor backgrounds or are refugees, join militias in order to get food, clothes, and a way to defend themselves.

FACT

In some countries, such as Colombia and Yemen, it is cheaper to buy a gun than a book.

VIEWPOINT

"It is immoral that adults should want children to fight their wars. There is simply no excuse for arming children."
Archbishop Desmond Tutu, South Africa

VIEWPOINT

"More children are able to become soldiers now because of new lightweight weapons, which are easy for children to handle."
Guardian newspaper, 1999

Child soldiers on an NPFL militia vehicle ride through the streets of Monrovia in 1996. Liberia's largest program to rehabilitate child soldiers had its resources looted during the fighting. Half the children chose to return to the streets and re-arm.

These children are both perpetrators and victims of violence. Between 1985 and 1995, conflicts killed about 2 million children and injured 6 million others. Those who survive often have their childhoods stolen from them and are left emotionally and physically devastated. The fallout from war affects all members of society in the countries involved. War usually means that health services and food and water supplies collapse. The resulting hunger and disease affect the young and the elderly the most. People are often forced to leave their homes. Sometimes families are scattered, and the children may be lost, orphaned, or abandoned.

Children and poverty

In India and parts of Asia and Latin America, street children are a common sight. With conflicts in Eastern Europe, such as those in the former Yugoslavia, they are also becoming more common on the streets of European cities like Bucharest and Sarajevo. Some are orphans. Others have been abandoned by families who are too poor or demoralized to look after them. They beg, comb garbage dumps for scraps, or work in restaurants earning only the food their employers give them. Some are forced into prostitution, and others work as couriers for drug dealers. They are often victims of violence and frequently get into trouble with the police. They are sometimes treated as "little more than vermin." Most of these children have no chance of any education, which is still the best way out of poverty. More than 130 million of the world's children, most of them girls, do not even attend elementary school.

A ten-year-old Cambodian land mine victim tries out her new artificial leg, which was provided by a British charity, The Cambodia Trust. Cambodia is one of the most heavily land-mined countries in the world.

Child labor

Traditionally, children in developing countries often worked with their families, learning skills they would need as adults. But now more and more children are forced to work for their own and their families' survival. They do exploitative, exhausting work in the fields, in makeshift factories, and in the households of the wealthy. Because of their age and more vulnerable position, employers find children easier to intimidate and cheaper to employ than adults. In India, children can earn between $98 and $123 per year, a significant amount for a family whose total annual income may be only $328.

A 14-year-old boy stitches soccer balls in his house on the outskirts of Sialkot, Pakistan's major sporting goods manufacturing city. The industry exports about 20 million soccer balls every year, but there are far fewer child workers since the major exporters in Pakistan signed an agreement with the International Labour Organization (ILO) in 1995.

In rural areas of Burkina Faso, children as young as 5 work to eat, many of them in unregulated goldmines where they are vulnerable to many dangers. They injure themselves with the heavy pickaxes they have to use. The "galleries" where they work sometimes cave in. Usually they work in dirty conditions without protection so they are also vulnerable to diseases such as cholera. The International Labour Organization (ILO) estimates that, worldwide, some 250 million children under the age of 15 work either full-time or part-time. And child labor is not restricted to less developed countries. An estimated 90,000 children

Some children work in factories, working long hours under harsh conditions, like these "aluminum children" photographed in Cairo, Egypt, in 1998.

between the ages of 8 and 14 work in the region around Naples in Italy. According to the United Nations Children's Fund (UNICEF), child labor flourishes because so many benefit from it, directly and indirectly:

- Employers exploit child workers and use their ready availability to force down adult wages.
- Governments benefit from increased exports and economic growth.
- Consumers at home and abroad enjoy lower prices of products.

Fortunately, there have been some successful attempts to limit or stop the use of child labor without removing the badly needed income that these children earn for their families. In 1995 UNICEF, the ILO, and the Bangladesh Garment Manufacturers and Exporters Association agreed to end the practice in Bangladesh and release children from the factories where they worked to attend special local schools. These children are paid a regular allowance each month, contributed to by the three organizations, to make up for their lost wages.

DEBATE

What do you think children's rights and responsibilities are? And how can people who are responsible for taking care of children try to ensure that they are happy, healthy, and safe?

VIOLENT CRIME

Throughout the world, murder is regarded as the most serious of crimes. It is also the easiest violent crime on which to get reliable statistics. Although murder cases receive a lot of coverage in the media, the global murder rate has gradually declined and is currently stable. Today most people in developed countries have a far greater chance of being killed in a car accident than being murdered.

It is more difficult to assess the extent of other violent crimes, such as assault and rape. Research suggests that there has been a steady rise in violent crime since World War II. But during the 20th century, the public became increasingly aware of certain types of violence that had previously

Many women are frightened to walk alone at night because they believe they risk being violently assaulted or raped.

attracted little attention or were not against the law. For example domestic violence and rape against women has long been reported, but male rape was not recognized in law until 1997.

In general, there has been a greater emphasis on crimes against people than on crimes against property. Experts suggest that crime statistics may not be a reliable source of information, because they only include crimes that are actually reported to the police. In the case of violent crime, it is believed that about one-third of victims choose not to contact the police, claiming that the attacks are a private issue.

Perpetrators of violent crime

The majority of violent criminals are young men who are likely to come from a background of poverty and live in inner cities. They are particularly connected with "street crimes" such as theft, burglary, assault, and rape, though the motivating factors behind each of these crimes is different. For example, rape of women is usually a violent expression of masculine power, dominance, and toughness; whereas the growing problem of "phone-jacking" (stealing mobile phones) probably has more to do with the increasing wealth of developed countries, where there are more valuables to steal.

Although statistics show that more women are getting involved in crime, their crimes (typically shoplifting, public drunkenness, drugs, and prostitution) rarely involve violence. As for children, since the 1990s it appears that there has been an increase in some violent crimes by children as young as ten. These are mostly boys, but an increasing minority of girls get involved in committing certain violent crimes. However, children are generally far more likely to be victims of violence than perpetrators.

VIEWPOINT

"'April, 29, 1994.
Dear Mr. Clinton,
I want you to stop the killing in the city. People is dead and I think that somebody might kill me. Would you please stop the people from deading. I'm asking you nicely to stop it. Do it now. I know you can.
Your friend
James.'
While walking home from a picnic with his family, James Darby, 9 years old, was brutally and senselessly gunned down in a drive-by shooting 9 days after writing this letter to President Clinton."
Joy D. Osofsky [ed.], Children in a Violent Society, 1997

FACT

In the United States, the number of violent crimes committed by teenages fell by nearly one quarter between the mid- and late-1990s.

Media commentators often claim that there is a "moral breakdown" among young people, pointing to things like vandalism, school truancy, and drug use in support of their case. However, some criminologists point out that young people have engaged in antisocial and criminal behavior throughout history, and their elders have always been outraged. These "moral panics" about youth criminality, they argue, may not accurately reflect reality.

Victims of violent crime

As well as carrying out the largest number of violent crimes, young, low-income, inner-city men are also the most common victims of theft, assault, and other forms of violence. When young men are members of minority groups they are even more likely to be targeted. This is because minority

People march in a gay pride parade in 1995. Although society is generally more tolerant of homosexuality than it used to be, many homosexuals still find themselves subjected to verbal abuse and violence.

groups, whether defined by race, gender, sexual preference, or class, tend to be viewed as a threat to society. Homosexuals, for example, experience a high incidence of violent crime and harassment.

Turning to crime

Why are young men from deprived backgrounds so much more likely than young girls from similar backgrounds to be involved in serious crimes? There are several possible reasons. One is that from an early age boys may join gangs in which crime is a way of life. Gangs can provide companionship, excitement, and a sense of belonging. Once gang members are labeled as criminals by the authorities, it is easy to continue down "the path of crime."

Another factor may be the rapidly changing position of men in society. In previous generations, young men could look forward to getting a job and taking on the role of father and breadwinner in the family. However, changes in the job market have made unemployment and job insecurity a real threat. Meanwhile, women are growing increasingly independent, both financially and emotionally. These changes in social and family structures have challenged traditional ideas about masculinity. Having a job is perhaps the most important legitimate way to gain respect in society. For a young man who has experienced a troubled, loveless childhood, the ability to earn a living can provide a sense of structure and stability in adulthood. Without this some will perhaps find other, more destructive ways of establishing a position for themselves in society.

VIEWPOINT

"Young men at the margins of society are particularly prone to violent fights and these mostly occur on the streets [around] where [they] live and also around bars and other places selling alcohol."
John Archer [ed.], Male Violence. *1995*

A group of young men hang out on the street in a small town. Boredom and frustration can lead some young people into vandalism and petty crime.

VIEWPOINT

"It does increasingly seem to be the view, particularly of the police, that prohibition is ineffective. It is wasteful of police time and alienates police and citizens so that in many western societies they feel like an occupying army. It leaves control of the drug to the underworld and makes it difficult to carry out effective drug education."
John Marks, Drugs Forum Trust, on legalizing marijuana

Almost all the world's coca plants and opium poppies, used to produce cocaine and heroin, are grown in developing countries such as Colombia. These members of a Colombian gang are involved in drug-related violence.

Violence and drugs

Illegal drugs are blamed for much of the increase in violent crime throughout the world. An illegal drug habit is expensive and addicts may use violence to get the money they need to buy regular supplies. Some drugs increase the chances of violence because they make people feel less inhibited. But many commentators argue that most of the violence associated with illegal drugs is really caused by the fact that the drugs are illegal. In 2002 the global drug trade was estimated to be worth up to $500 billion a year. This multibillion-dollar trade is controlled by organized gangs who engage in violent wars with each other to gain their share of the market. This keeps the price on the streets high and encourages people to risk their lives for profit.

As enforcement agencies begin to recognize that they are not winning "the war on drugs," critics of current drug policies suggest decriminalizing some so-called soft drugs such as marijuana. Others suggest a more radical approach. They argue that the most effective way to prevent the violence associated with the use of illegal drugs would be to start treating drugs as a social and health issue rather than a criminal problem, and provide treatment for those

who are addicted. Prices would fall and the drug barons and street gangs would go out of business.

Guns and gun control

In April 2002 a German student injured and killed 24 people at his college with several guns that he was licensed to have. He then killed himself. This shooting joined a growing list of multiple shootings that have horrified people everywhere. The killers are usually young males with grievances against society, school, or classmates. Most normal young people sometimes experience feelings of anger and resentment. When those young people have easy access to guns, such feelings can create a lethal combination. Despite passing some limited legislation to reduce the use of handguns, the United States continues to have the highest gun

Students from Columbine High School in Littleton, Colorado, wait for their friends to escape the building where two of their fellow students opened fire in April 1999.

ownership and correspondingly the highest annual number of gun deaths. Although adult murders have decreased since the mid-1990s, there has been a 58-percent increase in gun deaths of people under the age of seventeen since the early 1980s.

FACT

In the U.S. more family members are killed by one of their own family's guns—by accident, suicide, or an impulsive family fight—than are killed or even threatened by a criminal's gun.

While many people describe the increase in gun deaths as "an epidemic," members of pro-gun organizations resist changes to current gun laws. They insist that the Constitution grants them the right to bear arms in order to protect themselves. Other countries, concerned at the increase in both legal and illegal gun sales, have introduced tougher gun controls. In 1997 handgun ownership was banned in Britain. The ban, however, only appears to affect law-abiding citizens. In 1997 handguns were used in 2,648 crimes, but by 2000 there was a 40-percent increase to 3,685.

Two boys fight over a gun they have found in their father's bedroom.

Organized crime

Organized crime is a group enterprise that resembles a normal business but engages in illegal activities. Organized crime traditionally includes prostitution, smuggling (of drugs, goods, and people), illegal gambling, large-scale theft, blackmail, and intimidation. Because members of these groups rely on absolute secrecy within their organization, threats, violence, and bribes are commonly used to maintain discipline and loyalty.

Organized crime has become a multimillion-dollar business in the United States where it rivals the car industry in size. This type of crime has also become more sophisticated in its operation. Many criminal organizations have found ways of laundering "dirty money" (the proceeds of crime) by depositing it in big clearing banks. They then withdraw "clean money" and use it to set up legitimate businesses.

A masked, armed police officer leads a Moscow businessperson suspected of belonging to the Russian mafia.

Nearly every country has organized crime. There are Japanese yakuza, Chinese triads, Sicilian mafia, and most recently the Russian mafia, which some experts believe is the most dangerous organization of all. With computers and the Internet these organizations have become less territorial. They operate within flexible international networks, forming alliances between groups involved in different illegal trades such as weapons trafficking and the sale of nuclear materials.

Corporate crime

Corporate crimes are offenses committed by large companies and corporations. These increasingly powerful corporations touch our lives in many ways. They produce the food we eat, the drugs that combat our diseases, and the transportation we use. When these products or services cause injury or death, it is often extremely difficult to identify the individual responsible, so the whole company has to take responsibility.

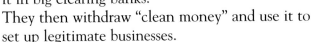

VIEWPOINTS

"If the person accosted by a criminal is likely to be armed, if the home owners are presumed to have guns, most criminals will think twice before mugging, raping or burglarizing …. you can't defend yourself with a gun control law."
From USA Today, 1993

"Statistics show that you are much more likely to be killed [in the U.S.] if you are carrying a gun than if you are not."
James Gilligan, Preventing Violence, 2001

FACT

In 2002 sixteen Austrian officials appeared before a Salzburg court charged with causing the mountain train inferno that killed 155 people in the tunnel leading to Kaprun on the Kitzsteinhorn glacier in November 2000. The train company admitted that there was no emergency plan in the event of a fire, and no fire extinguishers or hammers were in place.

FACT

Although Japan and the United States are the only democracies to keep the death penalty, Japan has a relatively low crime rate, while the United States has the highest murder rate in the developed world.

Corporate crimes may seem less obviously violent than crimes commited by individuals (like assault or murder), but they are often further-reaching in their consequences. For example, American car manufacturers believed their cars would not sell as well if they were fitted with seat belts, so their installation was delayed for decades, despite the evidence that seat belts would save thousands of lives. Similarly, British companies continued to expose their workers to asbestos long after its role in causing asbestosis (a fatal lung disease) had become known. All over the world, deaths from hazards at work far outnumber murders. Many of these deaths occur because companies ignore health and safety regulations.

Fears of violent crime

Whatever the facts, most people now believe that crime is more common and more serious. Surveys show that people are becoming more anxious about their homes being broken into and about being violently attacked. Women who have never been raped may be almost as fearful as those who have. They are often afraid of going out alone at night and may be equally afraid of staying at home alone. Many elderly people are confined to their homes, afraid to open the door to anybody.

The fact that serious crimes are widely reported in the media probably contributes to this perception of a worldwide "crime epidemic." There is also a belief that the police are less effective in preventing and detecting crimes. Unfortunately, one of the results of these fears is that more people, particularly young men, are carrying weapons for protection. This has been shown to increase the chances of serious injury or death. For example, in a confrontational situation with one or all of the participants possibly under the influence of drugs or alcohol, it is all too easy to pull out a knife or a gun.

Crime and punishment

When people break the law, they are arrested and charged by the police, then judged and punished by the courts. Most violent criminals are given prison sentences. The more dangerous the individual is considered to be, the longer the sentence. Prisons are supposed to punish criminals and also rehabilitate them (prepare them to return as honest members of society). Long prison sentences are thought by some to deter people from committing crimes, but their success is debatable. The United States, which has one of the world's harshest justice systems, also has, proportionately, the highest crime rate in the developed world.

DEBATE

State prisons do not seem to prevent crime and do not appear to adequately rehabilitate prisoners to face the outside world, what alternatives would you suggest, and why?

Death row inmate Genaro Comacho Jr. awaits execution in a Texas prison. He was executed on August 26, 1998, by lethal injection.

RACISM
AND VIOLENCE

What is racism?

Racism means treating people in a hostile or oppressive way because they belong to a different ethnic group. Such prejudice usually produces fear and antagonism between groups, and can easily turn into violence. For millions of people, in many countries, racial violence is a real threat in their everyday lives. It may take the form of name-calling, harassment, and abuse, and it sometimes leads to vicious racist attacks and murders. Racism often results in people of different ethnic groups being deprived of decent education, housing, and jobs.

Theories of race

Prejudice and discrimination have existed throughout human history. However, modern racism seems to have risen out of the exploitative relationship that Europeans established with nonwhite people in the 1700s. The slave trade could not have flourished without the widespread European belief that blacks belonged to an inferior race. Racism also helped to justify colonial rule over nonwhite peoples in such countries as Australia, New Zealand, and Africa during the 1700s and 1800s.

Count Joseph de Gobineau (1816–1882), sometimes called "the father of modern racism," proposed that white people possessed superior intelligence, morality, and willpower. These ideas influenced Adolf Hitler who transformed them into the ideology of the German Nazi Party, which was responsible for the murder of millions of Jewish and Romany people during the 1930s and 1940s.

After the British arrived in Australia in 1788, many of the native Aborigines were killed and their land was seized. Since the Native Title Act was passed in 1994, Aborigines, such as those pictured below, have been able to reclaim some of their land, but they still experience racism and are discriminated against in health, education, employment, and housing.

Since World War II "race science" has been thoroughly discredited. Experts now agree that there are no clear-cut biological differences between races, only a range of physical variations in human beings. Nevertheless white supremacist groups, such as the Ku Klux Klan and Aryan Nations in the United States, and Neo-Nazi groups in Europe, still firmly believe in the idea of racial superiority.

Ku Klux Klan members march in Houston, Texas, in 2000, when an African American, Garry Graham, was scheduled to be executed for the 1981 shooting of a white man.

The rise of fascist political groups

Individuals or gangs expressing the racist attitudes of their families or local communities commit many of the attacks on ethnic minority groups in the United States and Europe. There are thousands of racially motivated crimes every year in the United States. People from ethnic minorities are much more likely than white people to be the targets of an attack.

VIEWPOINT

"Human beings tend to fear, or at least feel cautious towards, anything or anyone very new or different. This may be natural, but it doesn't mean it's good or that human beings can't progress beyond these rather primitive emotions."
British Humanist Association

VIEWPOINT

"[Companies] don't give me a chance to prove I can do the job. At least 20 percent of it is being black. I know I can do the job."
Michael Oyeniyi, unemployed computer technician, 2000

Smoke rises from burning vehicles during rioting in Bradford, in the north of England, in July 2001. About 200 police faced thousands of Asian youths who threw gasoline bombs, bricks, and bottles in clashes triggered by far-right white supremacists' plans to hold a rally in the town.

The rise of extreme right-wing or fascist political groups, with their belief in the superiority of the white race, has alarmed many people. These far-right organizations believe that violence should be used against those they hate. They exploited the downturn in the global economy by encouraging those fearful for their jobs and quality of life to blame "foreigners" for unemployment and other social problems. In Germany, there were thousands of attacks on people the Neo-Nazis considered to be immigrants. In 1992, ten-year-old Yeliz Arslan, along with other members of her family, was killed in a firebomb attack on her house. Of Turkish origin, she had been born in Germany where her parents had lived for 23 years. Most Germans were appalled and many marched in protest.

In 2002 Jean-Marie Le Pen, leader of the extreme right French National Front, reached the final stages of the election for President. The French public, alarmed at this turn of events, voted in larger numbers than expected to block his election. In Britain the far-right British National Party (BNP) has had limited success in local elections, and Neo-Nazi groups have been implicated in some inner-city race riots.

Institutional racism

Some commentators argue that racism does not only exist among small groups of individuals. They suggest that racism is present throughout society's structures and institutions, including schools, police, and health care services. They claim that these

organizations promote policies that favor certain groups while discriminating against others. For example, in 1993 a black teenager named Stephen Lawrence, was killed by five young white people in South London. The fact that no one has been convicted of his murder has been seen as evidence of racism in the British police and criminal justice system. The shooting of Amadou Diallo in New York in 1999 raised similar concerns in the United States. Claiming to believe that Diallo, a Guinean immigrant, had a gun, the police shot him 43 times. The police authorities were strongly criticized for backing tough "law and order" policies that disproportionately targeted nonwhite New Yorkers.

Neville and Doreen Lawrence, Stephen Lawrence's parents. A 1998 government investigation found that the police had failed to conduct an adequate investigation in the hunt for Stephen's killers because the Lawrences were black.

Ethnic conflict

All over the world, people come into regular contact with other people who look different and perhaps also think and live differently. Some welcome this ethnic mix, while others find it dangerous and threatening. When there is competition for resources, employment, and housing, differences in language, religion, and culture may become exaggerated. In this situation, there can be suspicion, tension, and sometimes violence between the different ethnic groups.

Conflicts in the former Yugoslavia have involved attempts at "ethnic cleansing" (the forced removal of ethnic groups, usually using violence, threats, and harassment). The war in Kosovo in 1999 was prompted by charges that Serbians were ethnically cleansing the Kosovar Albanian (Muslim) population from the province.

Children pass Kosovar Albanian houses destroyed by Serbs during "ethnic cleansing" in 1999.

Genocide

The term "genocide" refers to the systematic elimination of one ethnic group by another.

The 20th century has seen the emergence of organized genocide, with the Holocaust being the most horrific example of planned extermination. In 1994 the ethnic Hutu majority in Rwanda launched a genocidal campaign against the ethnic Tutsi minority. Some 800,000 people were killed within three months, and 2 million refugees spilled over into Burundi and Zaire (now the Democratic Republic of the Congo).

Seeking asylum

In 2000 about 150 million immigrants were living outside their countries of birth. Of these, some 50 million people had been forced to leave their homes as a result of ethnic violence, racism, and racial discrimination. Most refugees either move within their own country or into neighboring countries, hoping to return to their homes when there is peace. Some, fearing imprisonment or persecution for racial or political reasons, seek asylum in other countries. Those who suffer from poverty migrate to try to find a better life for themselves and their families.

Many industrialized, developed states, fearful of being overwhelmed by different ethnic groups, have introduced tighter immigration controls. Negative and inaccurate portrayals of asylum seekers and refugees in the media and comments by politicians and public officials have contributed to the climate of hostility toward these groups. There has been an alarming rise in racist violence in Sweden, Britain, and Australia, including gang rape of refugee women.

Meanwhile, some asylum seekers and migrants, desperate to enter developed countries, pay large sums of money to smuggling syndicates who offer to help them avoid border controls. These arrangements are often extremely dangerous and can lead to tragedy.

VIEWPOINTS

"The overall picture that emerges from the recent press coverage is that asylum seekers are here [in the UK] to cheat us and take away from society."
Tony Kushner and Katherine Knox, Refugees in an Age of Genocide, *1999*

"Foreigners put 10 percent more into the system than they take out."
Home Office Department, Britain, 2001

Many countries now consider themselves "multicultural." How can the governments of such countries include ethnic minority groups and reduce racism? How do the cultures of different ethnic groups enrich communities?

POLITICAL VIOLENCE

VIEWPOINT

"No army in the world can stop an idea once its time has come."
Victor Hugo (1802-1885), French poet, novelist, and dramatist

Demonstrations and riots

In democratic countries individuals can vote for the government they want. But even in a democracy, people sometimes want to protest about government policies or support particular causes. In countries where people have basic rights of free expression, anyone can join in a peaceful protest, march, or meeting. But some people believe that the only way to attract attention for a cause is to use violence.

Through the centuries, people have demonstrated and rioted for a variety of political reasons, including unfair taxes, environmental concerns, land reforms, political and racial discrimination, and oppressive government policies.

Gagged (to represent their loss of freedom), Tibetan exiles stage a silent protest in Huairou, China, in 1995 against the Chinese occupation of their country.

Revolutions and invasions

Occasionally entire groups of people become so disillusioned by their country's political system that they deliberately use violence to overthrow an existing government. The French Revolution of 1789 and the Russian Revolution of 1917, both very bloody affairs, were extreme political protests. By comparison the "velvet revolutions," the overthrow of the communist systems in Eastern Europe and the former USSR since 1989, while no less dramatic, were much less violent. Revolutions attract great attention but in fact occur relatively rarely. Larger nations sometimes invade their more vulnerable neighbors and deprive them of their independence. In 1975, Indonesia annexed (took control of) East Timor. Protest movements in East Timor sought to achieve both independence and democracy. Many activists were imprisoned, tortured, or executed by their oppressors. In 1999 an Indonesian student-led demonstration forced President Suharto to resign. Several months later, the East Timorese voted overwhelmingly for independence from Indonesia. In 2001 democratic elections were held and the Independence Party (Fretlin), which had led the 24-year-long struggle for independence, was voted in.

Protesters hurl stones at Indonesian riot police in Jakarta in 1998. Several students died in clashes with the security forces during the unrest.

Violence by the state

People around the world are increasingly demonstrating for their right to live in peace with a government of their choice. But authoritarian regimes may use violence against their own populations to keep power and wealth in the hands of a very small group. In 1989 thousands of protesting students were killed in China's Tiananmen Square when the government crushed their movement for democracy.

The powerful monarchies in Saudi Arabia and Kuwait also strictly limit their citizens' civil rights and deny them any real participation in government affairs. Those who challenge the system may be obliged to escape, and join the increasing number of political refugees seeking asylum in more democratic countries.

FACT

In May 2002 the military junta that holds power in Myanmar released the pro-democracy leader, Aung San Suu Kyi, from house arrest. In 1990 the junta allowed elections. The National League for Democracy, of which Aung San Suu Kyi was co-founder, won 82 percent of the seats, but the junta refused to recognize the result and arrested all members of parliament. The junta is also accused of serious human rights abuses against their own people.

Terrorism

Terrorism usually refers to the deliberate killing of civilians in order to affect policies and laws. Terrorist acts of violence include bombings, hijackings, hostage-taking, assassinations, and threats against civilians. Although terrorism has existed throughout history, it began to achieve particular prominence during the second half of the 20th century. A desire to set up separate states within states has motivated the terrorist activities of such groups as the Basque separatists in Spain, the Tamil Tigers in Sri Lanka, and the Chechnyan rebels in southern Russia. Conflict between Israel and the Arab nations has also caused a great deal of international terrorist activity since the 1960s.

A woman is carried to an ambulance by emergency workers following a bombing by the militant Palestinian group Hamas at Jerusalem's Hebrew University in July 2002. The blast killed at least 7 people and wounded more than 80 others. Losses on both sides increase hatred and make it harder to find a solution to the conflict between the Palestinians and Israelis.

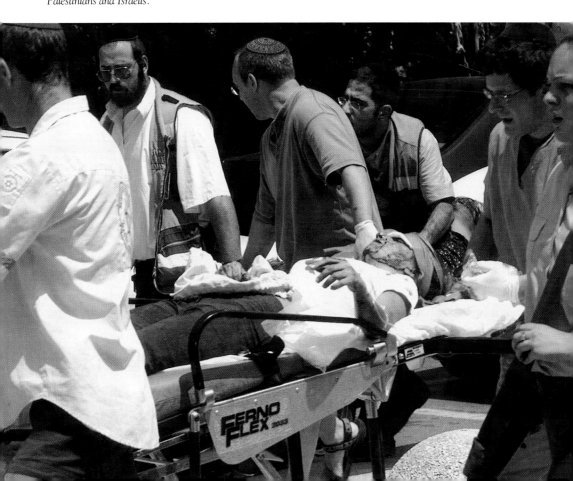

The rise of religious fundamentalism

As countries have modernized over the last two or three decades, some members of Christian and Islamic communities have become concerned about the undermining of many traditional values, including the importance of the family and a woman's so-called duty to obey her husband. Fundamentalism can be viewed as a desire to return to traditional social values and religious beliefs.

In some areas of the Islamic world this religious revival has been accompanied by a reaction against the impact of the more-developed world, particularly the United States. These sentiments are partly historical but they also spring from the continuing support the United States gives to Israel and its military presence in Arab countries. This antagonism has been demonstrated over the years by a number of terrorist incidents culminating in the attacks on the World Trade Center and the Pentagon on September 11, 2001. These attacks killed more than 3,000 people of all nationalities. Al-Qaeda, a loose network of terrorists headed by Osama Bin Laden, was considered responsible for what was viewed by all faiths and nationalities as a barbaric act against humanity.

The United States has seen the largest growth in Christian extremist movements, a few of which have been associated with violence. One of the best-known examples is the People's Temple. Their leader, Jim Jones, took about a thousand of his followers from California to establish a religious community in Guyana, South America. After a visiting U.S. Congressman was murdered, Jim Jones is said to have ordered his followers to commit suicide. More than 900 men, women, and children died at the Guyana settlement.

VIEWPOINT

"People who have been dispossessed, degraded, humiliated, but whose spirit has not been broken, understandably want to proclaim their grievances, whether or not they expect the proclamation to advance their cause.... The ones we call terrorists are the ones who have succeeded in that goal and used violence to succeed in it."
Annette C. Baier, Violence, Terrorism and Justice, 1991

DEBATE

If we want the world to become less violent, is violent protest ever justifiable?

VIOLENCE AS ENTERTAINMENT

The appeal of violence

Many individuals enjoy watching violent entertainment as long as they, the spectators, are not at risk. For example, the Romans enjoyed watching battles between gladiators, slaves who were forced to fight each other to the death. In modern times, this fascination encourages the media to focus on violence, whether it is in the reporting of world news or stories about murderers and serial killers on television, film, video, or in literature. Science fiction can also be extremely violent, with its depictions of alien creatures being

Young children watch a violent television show.

destroyed or waging war on humankind. In the light of all this, there is increasing concern about the effects of seeing so much violence. A 1992 study by the American Psychological Association claimed that the average American child or teenager viewed 10,000 murders, rapes, and assaults per year on television, with children's cartoons showing the highest number of violent acts. Research carried out over the last three decades suggests that watching screen violence for long periods of time may stimulate violent behavior in some vulnerable children and young people.

There are three main concerns about the effects of viewing violence. First, people could develop favorable attitudes toward violence because violent acts may be seen as an acceptable response to stress or anger. Second, by depicting violence as entertainment rather than as tragedy, these films or computer games could make viewers less sensitive to violence and the effects on its victims. Third, watching a lot of violence may encourage the belief that the world is as nasty and dangerous in real life as it is in television shows.

Reporting the news

The media also report on real-life events around the world. This may involve showing violence but its effects on the viewer are very different from the effects of watching a violent film or drama. Television broadcasters in particular accept that they have a duty to educate, to provide information about events, so that people can gain an understanding of the issues involved. For instance, wars—such as those in Kosovo and Afghanistan— have had extensive television coverage. But watching real violence being inflicted on other people, seeing the wreckage of homes and villages, horrifies many and may encourage people to find other ways to resolve conflicts.

VIEWPOINTS

"There have been allegations that Oliver Stone's movie, *Natural Born Killers* has inspired up to ten 'copy' killings. In Dallas, a 14-year-old boy decapitated [beheaded] a young girl after seeing the film and told friends he wanted to be famous like 'the natural born killers' in the movie."
Guardian *newspaper*

"It is as silly to blame a single film as it is to indict [accuse] the Bible, which forensic researchers have found to be the single most frequently quoted justification used by 'noble-cause' killers who murder prostitutes and homosexuals."
Guardian *newspaper*

DEBATE

Do you think watching violence influences violent behavior in any way? In a civilized society, should we still be entertained by violence?

VIEWPOINT

"...[G]ames and sports are one example of a safe and socially acceptable outlet for pent-up aggression."
Konrad Lorenz, On Aggression, 1963

Censorship

Many countries use rating systems with age restrictions or recommendations for admission to films that may contain violence. Because young people can get access to videos relatively easily, these are even more carefully censored. Sometimes more extreme scenes are cut entirely. In the United States and in Europe, television material considered unsuitable for children is shown later in the evening.

With the rise of the Internet it has become more difficult to control what people see. Many people think that violence and psychological horror should be limited in films aimed at the younger age group but that there should be a more relaxed attitude toward sex, nudity, and drugs. Anticensorship campaigners suggest a system that gives a rough guide to the content of entertainment and allows parents to decide what their children watch.

Violence in sports

Team sports often involve violence. Tension runs high, and tempers get frayed when there is a bad play or good results fail to materialize. Many critics fear that, in professional sports, violence is now becoming part of the game. In spite of condemnation by both players and the public, violent behavior is often tolerated. The media also plays a part. While appearing to condemn violent acts, it often pays considerable attention to them.

In some sports, such as football, huge amounts of money are paid to top players who attract large crowds and contribute a lot to their teams. While teams and coaches may

Ice hockey is popular in the United States but it can be a violent game. Here, a brawl breaks out after a Syracuse goal during a home game against the Kentucky Thoroughblades.

express dismay at violent behavior, they are often reluctant to reprimand such players.

There is also the problem of violence among fans. In Europe most soccer fans will express some friendly rivalry, but this can sometimes turn into violence. It has been suggested that Britain invented soccer, and later invented hooliganism. In fact other soccer nations, such as Brazil and Argentina, all have their own brands of hooliganism, including street fighting, vandalism, and drunkenness. In 1985 the behavior of a number of British soccer fans led to the deaths of 38 people, most of them Italian, at the Heysel Stadium in Belgium. As a punishment English soccer teams were banned for several years from playing in continental Europe.

A group of British soccer fans clash with local French teenagers in Marseilles, after England defeated Tunisia in 1998.

With better cooperation among police, soccer organizations, and fans, soccer violence has been significantly reduced since the 1980s. Known troublemakers have their passports siezed, rival fans are usually separated at matches, and alcohol is banned or discouraged.

Mike Tyson bites Evander Holyfield's ear during the WBA Heavyweight Championship fight in Las Vegas in 1997. Tyson was disqualified.

However, in some sports, such as boxing and wrestling, violence is the central theme. Boxers and wrestlers both try to injure each other, and a considerable number of boxers have been permanently injured or killed as a result of their fights. There have been calls for boxing to be banned, as it is in Sweden. However, defenders of the sport suggest that this would simply drive it underground where it would be impossible to monitor. They also point out that people choose to box; they are not forced to do so.

Killing for sport

Violence toward animals arouses a wide range of bitterly opposed opinions, especially when it comes to hunting. Some people argue that hunting deer and other animals for sport is the best way of keeping their numbers down. They suggest that the animal does not suffer during either the chase or the kill. Others claim that hunting is cruel and mainly carried out for the pleasure of the hunters. Antihunt demonstrators have staged many peaceful protests, but there have also been cases of violence and personal attacks on hunters to get their message across. This condemnation of killing for sport is a relatively recent phenomenon because people have become more aware of the number of animal species that are now threatened or endangered. For example, during the 1800s sportsmen from many countries went to India to hunt tigers. Now the tiger is one of the main examples of an animal that needs protection from human killers.

Other forms of violence against animals cause even more outrage. Dog fighting and cock fighting, for instance, are banned in many countries, yet both continue to flourish illegally. People bet on dogs or roosters that are made to fight until one is dead or too badly injured to continue. Poaching is another form of cruelty toward animals, often driven by the thriving trade in furs and in animal parts used in traditional Asian medicine.

VIEWPOINTS

"So far all our financial and human resources have had to go into defending hunting and this makes us appear very reactionary. In an ideal world, the currently hostile government would give us five years in which to find out what changes would make hunting more acceptable to the wider public and then to implement them."
Michael Sagar. Horse and Hounds magazine. 2001

"People are abusing, tormenting, and killing [rabbits] for the fun of it, and this depravity should have no place in the Britain of 2001."
Robert Jackson. Observer newspaper. 2001

Bullfighting, an ancient and violent Spanish custom, usually ends in death for the bull and can also be extremely dangerous for the bullfighter. Here, Jose Luis Parada bleeds after being gored during the traditional April bullfighting fair in Seville in 1995.

PREVENTING VIOLENCE

Keeping the peace

At the end of World War II, there was a determination that the devastation of two world wars must never happen again, and the United Nations (UN) Organization was established to work for peace and international cooperation. The UN includes the United Nations Children's Fund (UNICEF) which works to protect children and young people from violence and abuse all over the world.

Many national governments, along with the UN and other international bodies such as the International Criminal Court in the Hague, are trying to find ways of ending collective violence in all its forms, including genocide, war crimes, racial discrimination, and ethnic cleansing. In 1996 the South African government set up the Truth and Reconciliation Commission to examine the abuses that had occurred under apartheid. The hearings were not intended to be trials or to assign blame, but to acknowledge the injustices in an atmosphere of humility and open debate.

The world's wealthier nations are also starting to recognize that poverty and violence are interlinked, and that they have an obligation to reduce poverty and increase economic opportunities in the poorest nations. In 2002 the United States and the European Union provided debt relief for 24 of the world's poorest countries but only on the condition that they put all the money into health care, education, and development.

Starting from the beginning

People can "learn" to be violent if they experience violence at a young age. Children who consider hitting to be normal are more likely to bully and use violence in later life. In 1989 a major campaign was launched to help organizations all over the world to end all physical punishment of children. This includes not only spanking but also the more extreme forms of violence such as beating and capital punishment. In 2000 the National Society for the Prevention of Cruelty to Children (NSPCC), set up the "Full Stop" campaign, which hopes to eliminate child abuse by 2020. The NSPCC tries to prevent abuse occurring in thefirst place by encouraging all members of the community to take some responsibility for reporting it. In cases where children and young people have been abused, the NSPCC provides therapy to help them recover, making it less likely that they will abuse their own children.

A Brazilian boy learns to use the Internet at a school run by a nonprofit organization in a shanty town in Rio de Janeiro, in 2001. The parents of the poorest families are paid to send their children to school.

VIEWPOINT

"The only way to get kids not to hurt each other is to get kids not to want to hurt each other."
Adrian LeBlanc. "The Outsiders." New York Times Magazine

As poverty is being recognized as a factor causing increased abuse and violence in families and communities, governments need to set up programs that give poorer families financial and social support. Preschool educational and family support programs have been shown to reduce delinquency (law-breaking) and crime later in life. Once children are at school, programs teaching them how to resolve conflicts peacefully also appear to reduce the rate of future violence.

For several years, police in Boston have successfully applied a community policing and prevention approach to criminality in youth gangs. While stating very clearly that they would crack down firmly on all crime, they have also offered rehabilitation programs for alcohol and drug

Children attend a peace and reconciliation class supported by UNICEF in Burundi, 1995.

addicts, and further education. Making education and employment accessible is one of the most effective and successful means of preventing violence.

What can you do?

Societies can only become less violent if we all recognize that it is possible to live our lives in a nonviolent way. Some experts put this idea more forcefully: Unless the human race takes steps to prevent violence, we may not survive this century.

- **How you and your friends live your lives can make a difference.**
  Home should be a safe place. If you know of anyone who is experiencing violence or abuse at home, tell someone in authority that you trust— a parent or teacher. Do not agree to keep it a secret. Abusers count on secrecy.

- **Schools should encourage nonviolent attitudes.**
  If someone else is being hurt by bullies, don't stand by and let it happen. If you are putting yourself at risk, get help. Tell the victim that you want to help and encourage friends and classmates to do the same. Find out about your school's anti-bullying policy. Is it an effective policy or do you and your friends know of other nonviolent procedures that you think would reduce bullying? Tell other young people about these.

There are many organizations that work to prevent violence (see Useful Addresses, page 60). You might like to join a local group, or organize a fundraising event. Remember, your voice counts. There is a Chinese proverb that says, "A journey of a thousand miles begins with a single step." If each of us takes a step to change attitudes and practices, the world will become a safer and happier place.

FACT

After 19 years of violence that left some 64,000 people dead, the rival sides in Sri Lanka returned to the negotiating table. In February 2002 the Tamil Tigers signed a ceasefire with the Sri Lankan government and agreed to meet for peace talks mediated by Norway.

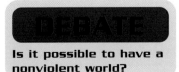

DEBATE

Is it possible to have a nonviolent world?

GLOSSARY

adultery sexual relations between a married person and someone other than the person's husband or wife

annex to take control of another country or state

apartheid meaning "apartness," a system of government introduced in South Africa in 1948 to keep black, white, mixed-race, and Asian people separate and unequal

assault to attack violently; a violent attack

asylum seeker someone who suffers because of his or her skin color, culture, religion, or political beliefs, and flees to another country to seek asylum (a safe haven). Asylum also means the right to live in another country if you have been attacked for one of these reasons.

authoritarian government that emphasizes harsh enforcement of rules and laws

capital punishment lawful punishment by death; otherwise known as execution or the death penalty

censor to examine and remove anything considered to be offensive in films, books, etc.

civil war a war between citizens of the same country

coercion persuasion by force

colonial rule control over people or areas, historically used by European countries such as Britain, France, Spain, and Portugal, to dominate countries in Africa, Asia, and the Americas

corporal punishment physical punishment, such as hitting or spanking

courier (in the drugs trade) someone who carries illegal drugs from one country to another

criminologist someone who studies criminal behavior

delinquency behavior, especially by young people, that goes against accepted social standards or breaks the law

democracy a political system in which citizens elect their own rulers and take part in decision-making

deprived without food, money, or comfortable living conditions

developed countries the wealthier countries of the world, including those of Europe, North America, Japan, Australia, and New Zealand. People living there are normally healthy, and well educated, and often work in a variety of high-technology industries.

developing countries the poorer countries of the world including much of Africa, Asia, and Latin America. People living there are often unhealthy and poorly educated, and work in agriculture and lower-technology industries.

domestic violence term used to describe violence within a family setting, usually between adults

dowry money or goods traditionally given by a bride's family to the bridegroom at marriage. Most commonly practiced in India, it is now illegal there, but the custom continues.

economy the system by which a country's wealth is produced and used

ethnic cleansing the policy of forcing the people of a particular ethnic group or religion to leave an area or country

ethnic group a group of people who share a common culture, tradition, and sometimes language

fascist someone who obeys one powerful leader, opposes democracy, and believes that his or her country or ethnic group is better than all others

fundamentalism the practice of following the traditional rules of a religion, such as Christianity or Islam, very exactly

gender classification by male or female

genocide the deliberate killing of an entire ethnic group or nation

globalization growing social and economic interdependence between different peoples and countries in the world

harassment repeated verbal or physical attacks

heterosexual someone who is sexually attracted to people of the opposite sex

homicide murder

homosexual someone who is sexually attracted to people of the same sex

hooliganism noisy, rough, aggressive behavior, sometimes associated with soccer fans

Hutterite member of the Anabaptist sect who came from Eastern Europe during the 1800s to escape religious persecution

ideology a set of ideas, especially one on which a political or economic system is based

International Labour Organization (ILO) a UN organization that investigates working conditions around the world and proposes legislation to protect workers from abuse and hazards in the workplace.

intimidate to bully, threaten, or frighten

junta a government (especially a military one) that has come to power by force rather than through elections

masculinity qualities traditionally considered typical of a man, such as strength, self-reliance, and the ability to support a family

minority group group of people in a society who are set apart from the majority population by their physical or cultural differences. Minority groups often experience hostility and unfair treatment from larger groups

National Society for the Prevention of Cruelty to Children (NSPCC) British charity that is concerned with children's welfare

pedophile adult who is sexually attracted to young children

perpetrator someone who does something wrong or criminal

post-traumatic stress disorder condition of mental stress, anxiety, and sometimes physical illness which may follow injury or psychological shock

rape to have sex with someone against their will

refugee someone who has been forced to leave his or her country for political reasons or to escape a war

rehabilitate to help someone find ways of fitting into society (e.g. when coming out of prison), through education, retraining, new employment, or therapy

syndicate group of people or companies combined together for a particular purpose, usually business

therapy treatment of physical or mental disorders without using drugs or surgery

zero-tolerance policy approach to crime prevention that emphasizes maintaining order by targeting small-scale crime and minor disturbances in order to prevent more major crime problems

BOOKS TO READ

Armitage, Ronda. *Talking Points: Family Violence*. Chicago: Raintree, 2000.

Barbour, Scott (ed.). *Teen Violence*. Farmington Hills, Mich.: Gale Group, 1998.

Gedatus, Gus. *Guns and Violence*. Minnetonka, Minn.: Capstone Press, 2000.

Goldentyer, Debra. *Preteen Pressures: Street Violence*. Chicago: Raintree, 1998.

Stewart, Gail B. *Guns and Violence*. Farmington Hills, Mich.: Gale Group, 2001

Torr, James D. (ed.). *Current Controversies: Violence in the Media*. Farmington Hills, Mich.: Gale Group, 2000.

USEFUL ADDRESSES

Amnesty International
322 8th Avenue
New York, NY 10001
Tel: 212-807-8400

Coalition to Stop Gun Violence
1023 15th St. SW, Ste. 600
Washington, DC 20005
Tel: -202-408-0061

Family Violence Prevention Fund
383 Rhode Island St., Ste. 304
San Francisco, CA 94103-5133
Tel: 415-252-8900

National Domestic Violence Hotline
PO Box 161810
Austin, TX 78716
Tel: 800-799-SAFE

UNICEF
3 United Nations Plaza
New York, New York 10017
Tel: 212-326-7000

Violence Policy Center
1140 19th St. NW, Ste. 600
Washington, DC 20036
Tel: 202-822-8200

INDEX

Numbers in **bold** refer to illustrations.

INDEX